ACKNOWLEDGEMENTS

KU-354-908

Some of these poems have appeared in the following magazines and anthologies:
Northwords, Poetry Scotland, Fife Lines, The Red Wheelbarrow, The Rialto, The Broken Fiddle, Pushing the Boat Out, Where the Land Meets the Sea, (edit. Tom Bryan), *Things Not Seen* (edit. Stuart B. Campbell), *The Herald, New Writing Scotland, Chapman.*

Original Myths, with etchings by Paul Fleming, was published in book form by Cruachan Publications, Portsoy, in 2000.

"All Things want to fly. Only *we* are weighed down by desire, caught in ourselves and enthralled with our heaviness."

(Rilke, *Sonnets to Orpheus*, 2·14, translated by Stephen Mitchell.)

BLIZZARDS OF THE INNER EYE

Blizzards of the Inner Eye

IAN CROCKATT

Lydia —
Write on !
Ian

PETERLOO POETS

First published in 2003
by Peterloo Poets
The Old Chapel, Sand Lane, Calstock, Cornwall PL18 9QX, U.K.

© 2003 by Ian Crockatt

The moral rights of the author are asserted in accordance with the Copyright,
Designs and Patent Act, 1988

All rights reserved. No part of this publication may be
reproduced, stored in a retrieval system, or transmitted,
in any form or by any means, electronic, mechanical,
photocopying, recording or otherwise without the prior
permission in writing of the publisher.

**A catalogue record for this book is available
from the British Library**

ISBN   1-904324 - 07-X

Printed in Great Britain by
Antony Rowe Ltd, Chippenham, Wilts.

Contents

THE CLEFT HEART

Concert, With Love

A glass of minims,
tremulous and transparent
as fragments of water;

baton-straight crochets
marching under their helmets
across fields of snow;

a cuffed and collared
perfectionist cracking ivory
fingers bone by bone; then

Love, strong as the song
on her ululating tongue,
in the sanctum of her mouth –

I offer my cleft heart up
to you, beating like applauding
palms, bruise-blue.

Dwarf Birch

'He's one who, skirting this waste of land,
saw me and thought *poor cliché* –
roots in a rock-cleft, stars for blossom,
as much use as a plough in a city.'

She seemed to spread her lichened palms
and shrug in disbelief – 'am I
so deformed? What of it? Why should a birch
with a hump wedged between moor and sky

not be loved? Far from your plumped-
up urban shrubberies with their dangly
laburnums and strangled beeches,
their gorgon-haired sycamore-clumps

and lather of fruit-bruised bushes,
love flourishes; yes, honed to its last
flung leaf but what of that? If it pushes
me over the mind's veined edge so be it.'

She cried. 'He passed me – I lost all grip –
like a bee deflowering flowers, a treasure-ship.
Without kisses from his pollen-dusted lip
I'll die, and then who'll shoulder this sky?"

As Into a Blue Lochan

Between the hard sides of mountains
lie the soft-lit waters
of your eyes in their bony bowls,
blue-grey, breeze-dimpled.

After the long climb you let me
strip to the sweating skin,
step from the rim as into a blue lochan
and, at last, swim.

Fishes disguised as rainbows
lead me to the mountainroots where nerves
of lazing weed transform light –
your dreams stream by like pictures.

I catch them quick as smolts in my bare hands,
muscular, scaly, slimed,
primed for the ocean's trials of strength to come,
their miraculous returnings,

and my hands recall to me those primitive female
pulsings which make men come,
there in the blue-lit deepnesses of your eye
between granite-hard mountains.

Brackened slopes fall to pale rock-slabs
wavering under the water.
Resurfacing is like looking again in your eyes –
the so welcoming starred blue sky

caressing the world at its centre – as if I
were not just the mountains
stretching up but, honed to the peak of hardness
and leaping in you, a salmon in all its prime.

Or Not To Be

I want to be engulfed

by love; its scouring breakers
upending me, its faithful pools
netting moons in my hair.

I've got to

break out of this skin
these flesh-lumbered limbs
the sarcophagus of the air

and be

elemental – the wind,
a mercury-drop.
I've come this far – now

let my mind be

tight as a walnut, cool
as a tightrope-walker's
stepping from star

to star

over light-year drops;
all time behind him,
this longing to turn back

stopped.

5.00 a.m.

Sweet, the night is short
and the long yawn of tomorrow is mustering its greys.
Folded, opening, spread like maps
our bodies travel each others' unuttered ways.
The vole encounters the hawk;
tongue to tongue we talk.

Your limbs are silver birches
your mouth is a dripping hive
your hair is the silk wind binding me –
I am so alive;
oh and we have ridden
the muscled mares of night to exhaustion!

Butter-skin, well-throat,
what does day mean? Century-long
hours in mental tower-blocks, feeling's
oneway systems potholed and clogging.
Where will our flying hooves spark
furnaces like these kisses in the dark?

We both know how this will end.
Give me one last interminable night
clutching you to my heartbeat like a bomb.
Don't let's lose sight
of our beginnings – small touchings, dumb glances, plumbed
meanings – when day's fixed bayonets come.

Fallen Angel

I can't stop listening for that light step in the hall,
the penultimate footfall

of my pacing angel,
halo drawn tight as a virgin's bangle,

unholy desire in her eyes.
I won't flinch or act surprised

when she breaks scythe-winged through the door –
it's me she's fallen for.

Understand that I choose
her caresses' lacerations, her kisses' radiant bruises –

and that these are my last bequests;
the salt-lick of her brow, the dew of her breasts,

and, slipping through my fingers, this melt-pool of gold,
plosive as rocket-fuel, deep-space cold.

Evening Walk

Honed hills fan out round us
like a gang, barely retreating.
The river twists and turns on sunset's

spit. Sweet hive
of the fallow field, my speaking heart,
when sky comes stooping over

to defend us you be Moon –
cast your light nets; I'll be Jet
and scorch their skulls –

these are not the first to fear
the transforming zealotry
of our love.
                    Missile-silos brimming

with autumn rust, radar-dishes
homing in on larks. As clouds
trail their skirts across the hills –

darknesses retreating through the dark –
our minds ball and swarm
and the honeycomb fills. Let's never part.

Taking More Than the View

We're lying on top of Scotland
taking more than the view.

Love is one last gasp away
from completion, as if

an eagle had gripped
its soft-furred prey and risen

on thermals high as Beinn Niebheis –
then dropped it. Bleeding

and turning in the pummelling wind
it plummets to that moment –

now – of merging with rushing tundras,
when eagles' unfaltering

sky-wide wingspans
fold, and the longed-for smack

of impact splits the love-
prey open from thigh to throat.

We are two felled white stalks
of flesh on the rim of a lochan;

our hearts are a tumult
of scarlet muscle; Scotland's too.

She raises up her head
and inhales cloud from the Atlantic.

She rolls from beneath us,
massive-fleshed, strong, breathing out snow.

Miss Scotland 1998

Then she lay like a woman bathing,
allowing the Atlantic and the North sea
to break themselves on her.

Her languages were the relics
of migrant clans driven by raiding tribes
to rape and subdue her.

Some still came with plums in their mouths
speaking as if forced marriage
were the making of her.

She was more beautiful than the diamonds
forming the driven tips
of the needles inserted in her

to draw off rich oils,
but lay pliant in the shallows
letting them bleed her.

Why couldn't we rouse her?
Her breath is purer than a corrie's,
her mouth is sweeter than a lochan's –

was it the passiveness of her beauty
stopped us embracing her?
But now when she flutters that sinuous

tongue, with its many-coloured lilts,
we are mad with love and indiscretion –
it's time to stand erect beside her

to pluck the diamonds from her veins
cut the dull gold from her finger,
and unleash the deluge of her hair.

Walking to Cape Wrath

And there, amongst thin grasses,
stood toadstools, dainty phalli,
the laceworked lingerie
of slub-silked fungi – erect,
lum-reek subtle,
right in your eye; out there

on the rim of delight
where flesh confronts its weakness
like a thousand-mile old wave
shagged out by its travels,
fumbling ashore.

Willow

There is a green-plumed tree,
a whip-limbed swayer,
bowed over an iron frame,
bell-plump and shady.

It sifts notes like leaves
– dark crochets, pale quavers –
thrums the drum-taut air
with percussionist's fingers.

Summoned in we push through
swung resonating skirts
to its one ribbed limb –
drive all elbow and knee

in, in beyond each other,
urgent as sucking young,
sperm mobbing the egg –
like arriving in a shimmering

laceworked tent, pressing
into the mother of petticoats
crying, "me, choose me,
love me above all others."

Love Sequence

1.
You can't see it like the steam out of drains
when the city's vascular system overheats;
it's odourless as the methane off a pond
purpling under its weed-crust; it's unstoppable
as lava out of the earth's parched throat; it's
more like a bullet's arrival than like gunsmoke.

And it's alive – symbiotic, painful, warming –
there are fever symptoms, irrationalities.
An illness half like this would consume corpuscles
or multiply like a tumor. Both toxic and sweet-
mouthed it is inspired like poetry, but can't be
exhaled like words on the breath. It causes
fixations, obsessions, hallucinatory joy;
turned this reasonable man into a desperate boy.

2.
Imagine there is no anger
despite her treatment of your heart –
just this blue marsh-mallowed sky;
yet every twig in the forest, your
broad-leafed paradise, is taut to its tip –
it's as if the very air, reeking of her
perfumes, electric with desire,
had sapped your capacity to weep.

Your heart bobs soft as cloud
and you seem to hear its thunder
– of submission, never anger –
as you close your shadowed eyes,
as she spills her hair like blood across
the fungal paleness of your thighs.

3.
Moth, my moth, more leaf than moth
in your camouflaged fatigues,
half-glimpsed in half-lit flight
beneath a moon-drenched mesh of leaves,
pity this fumbling man clubbing the air
with rifle-butt and barrel as he writhes
in leaf-mould slime at the forest's foot –
a pit for his stomach, well-holes for eyes,
mouth waterless as the moon, dumbed, petrified.

Moth, my moth, leaf-light, mouth-soft,
flitting kiss-like from throat to cringing balls,
secreting seed like mines in creases and pores,
what stops you?
How long before this flesh succumbs
to your hordes' insatiable jaws?

4.
She dreams we have to find the promised dead,
our bird-limbed, fish-finned originals.
We're caving or diving – no, excavating tombs,
tweezering through rubble, tantalised by shards;
but where are the artifacts sensationalists crave,
and that rumoured room-within-a-room
adventurers have vanished from like pharoahs?

Discovering neither statuary nor bones
we crawl (she dreams) towards the sun, stumble
parch-lipped out of the burgled valley
with nothing to report but claustrophobia,
myth-beasts spirited from their crumbling niches,
our faces averted and one-dimensional,
marriage vows reduced to hieroglyphs.

5.
And love keeps intervening like a referee,
getting thumped but pushing in again,
insisting on being the no-man's land we
score between us after each offensive;

while the parents of this poppy-spattered boy
beg him to throw in the towel but over
the top he goes, no more than their big bruised boy
blundering into a future they don't know;

and this minister fluttering his hanky
over our stretchered lives – while bullets
snub their noses on pavements and bone –
until some final whistle is blown.

And what shall lovers do? In this suit of blood-
stained words am I naked enough for you?

Table for Two

Stop doing embroidery in your head.
Silence will prove pregnable,
though spread now like a linen sea
ironed to the cutglass horizon
over which it falls silently.

Is Bayeux your home? Are you
descended from the Lady of Shallot?
I have you under siege, arrows
and lances of uproar swarming in,
your cutlery armies reeling –

and you weaving signs with your hands
like a tranced Noh dancer. Waiters
dart like feeding dragonflies,
columns of sound form arches be-
tween which I hear cries splashing –

lives beyond starched tablecloths,
big wet tides of emotion
unknown to sipped-at glasses. Oh
lower the nimble drawbridge of your tongue,
make words walk its plank and drop

into the whirlpool of my ear! She
smiled. I could see the embroidery un-
ravelling as I spoke, spilling across
the table, flocking our clothes. Her hand
arrived at my cheek, tore like a rose.

Reaching for Each Other

Not a star in night's dark hood.
The town waits with its head in a fog,
the breath of every chimney at its throat.
Nothing except the fingers and eyes

of the Internet surfers moves,
and the hearts deep in them leaping
to the tunes of unknown others.
Skyczar 1 and Yakstar

coo over each others' names,
conjuring feelings. Is there any
darker pit than dreamt-up truths –
or lightning brighter? Their longings

filter through binary codes,
the soft clickings and swishings
of P.C.s searching themselves
for deeper meanings. What can it mean

when Skyczar's E-mail says
luv u 2 and Yakstar's screen drips
tears in a boxroom under the eaves
of some fog-blurred suburb?

There is too much to grasp
as the humans reach for each other
in screen-hushed rooms. No owls, not
even one star in night's dark hood.

The Lily and the Book

And when the lily lifts
her trumpet from the grasslands
and blows true notes,
so high and pale and flickery
they out-blink the visible stars,

whole libraries of words
spill to the floor and shape
themselves new meanings –
heart-syncopated poetry, treatisies
on the astronomies of love.

And when she bares her yellow stamens,
proffers them to the sun
and the hunting bee, each book spreads
its print-veined wings and explicates
its pollen-dance, for me. The lily

gifts to this book frail
sensual equivalents of its phrases,
each translating her vivid-scented morse;
and when she lives between these pages
kisses underwrite my rashest words.

But are they more than the lexicon
of an intoxicated brain? Don't
read me like a book, literally;
as stars beyond our senses move the stars
we've names for, she moves me.

THE SECOND COMING

Shards for a Maker

Bind me a boat of Nile reeds
to ferry a cargo of prophets
to the silting delta, this Moses

to his tribe, that child to his father.
Shape me a swan of the Lower Nile,
a great white-winged felucca,

the fruit of the fields in its crop
for Pharoah's larder. Carve me a dhow
of gopher-wood with many-coloured sails

to transport the jealous hearts
of Joseph the Dream-teller's brothers.
Mould me of Upper Nile clay

an Ark, fired in a thousand riverbank
kilns, decks of red oxide and bulwarks
glazed green, to house two by two

each species extinguished since Eden –
the Lost-in-Death, the Stolen-from-Life
of all eras. Set it as an icon

on Mount Ararat, the cemetery
of the world, a petrified dove
with its fruitless twig fused to the deck -

house roof. Make shards from its rainbow
ribs for the Seers to ponder over.
And bind me a Nile reed-boat. Remember?

The Tay

bridge

where spring-tides greet pale
stonework's engineered beauty –
thighs in the torrent

estuary

moon-bathing sandbanks
sleekit as pearl-divers' limbs
resurfacing, gone

sailboats

and the fleet a wood
all at sea, keel-roots groaning
veined sails bulging – free

squall

struck – tore the skyline
from its hinges, forced our port-
holes under; foam, sea

the return

sssh – ghost-sails slatting,
low foghorn's breathing; the boat-
hook kissing the buoy

Kelp

(after a photograph by Orlando Galtieri)

Observe. In this gleam-lit leatherwork shop
amongst the clutter of flung-down bridles,
head-collars, whips and saddlery, there hangs

a tawse. Polished and supple, yes, but
slack-hanging down; old fork-tongue's out
of its element. Which was the winter-dulled

classroom of Primary 6, year nineteen
fifty seven, that time it convulsed and spat
from Miss MacCreadie's fist, splitting my palm.

Her stiff, white papier-mâché face made
no sound. The tawse rose like a striking snake
and struck, crack, again. She made no sound.

Years later we heard she'd drowned – out
of her depth too, ill-adapted for water.
I pictured her glide through the kelp-forest –

its current-swung boughs, its slippery lives –
her hands pale flounders, limbs like languid eels,
papier-mâché dissolving noiselessly.

She'd a passion for horses and we'd had to
draw them – mine were loll-tongued sea-monsters.
"That's what you see?" she'd snapped, "I'll teach you to see!"

Observe. In this gleam-lit leatherwork shop
you see Miss MacCreadie's tawse, slack-hanging down.
Now try to catch her hands before they're gone.

The Dunes in Moon's Head

(from a photograph called "sand detail", by Orlando Galtieri)

Pity that old moon,
pock-faced, alone, sculpting his self-
portrait in shadow and sand.

Dreaming of young flesh
at the world's beginning, he
called it Desire. Addicted

to skin he saw clay
thighs meet like continents, clench
with the shuddering movement

of warmed land-masses. Millenia
passed, discarding re-
dundant peoples. In moon's head

each toppled dome and
minaret of their buried cities
teemed with young-limbed women.

He reached out fingers
of light and in the dune-shaded
pits of their arms, the oases

of their bellies, a-
long the soft-fleshed wadis of
their spines, buried himself; so making

his funeral mask – this blueprint
for those, he said, compelled
to excavate their own heads.

The Fear

Certain when blasted by mania
that I can spin 10 planets on one fingertip
and peripheral paraphernalia
like families, nations and galactic relationships

will settle, as the slowing planets teeter,
into perfected mind-sized spaces;
but sweat-soaked by this reasonless fear –
that the whole scaffolded edifice

of my rocket-inspired mind-tower,
its epic cathedral proportions, the sun-
orbiting potential of it all, might falter,
one microchip fail, my sky-high High cut down

by some earthed brain-clotting thought;
and hope, frail nerve-lit star so innocently formed –
oh do not dream it –
metamorphosed to this dark, deranging poem.

Dear Mr. Crichton Smith

Dear Mr. Crichton Smith,
how our languages mourn you.
Though the cottages on Kerrera Sound
are stoical in their grief
the lilt in the Minches' mouths
and the songs in the eyes of the lochans
moored in Lewis' peat
fade like exiles.
And when the west wind stoops
who comforts the east-bowed tree?

Dear Mr. Crichton Smith
our languages have linked hands
to chorus your eulogy –
steering your clinker-built word-boat
beyond the harbour wall,
circumnavigating the speechless world,
what were you dreaming of?
What tidal wave found you?

The sea is an anarchy of grief;
dear Mr. Crichton Smith
did you never wish yourself cow-dumb;
not double-blessed, not
shaken by poem-speak?

Visiting Vartifoss

(a waterfall in Southern Iceland which has eroded the lava and soil of the cliff if falls over
reveal a gleaming amphitheatre of basalt columns. *Hallsgrimskirkja*, named after a celebrat
poet, is a superb modern church in Reykjavik housing a silver-piped organ)

Where is the organist of Hallsgrimskirkja?
Here are his columns of fluted pipes,
and his basalt-limbed choristers craning
their lava necks to mouth lost chants –
Timor mortis conturbat me.

And here is their basso counterpoint,
this flung tail-end
of ice-melt falling froth-
white to its nemesis – spittle
from under a glacier's tongue,

the churned ice and fire
of dropped gutturals and dipthongs
thick on its lips as morraine.
Hallsgrimskirkja of pre-history,
cathedral of whitest air absorbing

our syllables like light,
your lichen-lipped organ is building notes high,
higher within me than prayer;
and every bone of me – perfectly pitched
as water poured into itself –

instinctively spouts hosannahs.

The Commission

"Shape me a suite of voluptuous chairs
framed with Beech and Walnut exceedingly
Richly Carved in the Antich manner and Gilt
in oiled Gold, the whole stuff'd and cover'd
with glibbest Crimson Damask. Let the Castors
on their gold-shagged feet be strong, fit
to carry a Tassled and Ermine-cloaked King
and sundry stiff-wigged Lordships should He
and They so deign. Be sure to make each
wide as the Royal Buttocks, and to spare, all
amply squabb'd and curlicu'd with Gesso and Gold-
leaf patterns – incorporating Pegasae with young
girls' curl-hung heads – so Artfully and Costlily
arranged as to assure Ten Generations there are
none Lovelier or more Rare – "

And still we could not match, despite his Lavished
Millions, the living pinks and goldens
of his chambermaid's cheeks and hair.

NOTE: The original commission of 1794, and invoice dated 7th July 1765, of Lord
Dundas' order for 8 large Armchairs and 4 large Sophas designed by Robert Adam and
made by Chippendale – total £510.4.0 – are still extant. Some of the Chairs and a Sopha
can be seen at Duff House, Banff. Other were recently sold, each of the chairs making in
excess of 1 million pounds.

Give Me Excess of It

I love it when the guitar-bird
stretches its neck and calls, takes off
in a welter of wing-notes

for the cymbal-clashing spheres; and I
can't resist the feathery flights
of the plump-hipped viola-fowl,

or the brassy pheasant-horn
trumpeting alarms across the fields,
or a swan-necked flute's descanting refrain.

But best is their massing to migrate,
those honks and squawks as they prepare
for the orchestrated dreamscape of flight –

instinctively internationalist, driven
to the air by compulsion,
need, blood-knowledge; vision beyond sight.

Goose-pimples gather in flocks
on my listening skin; border guards
striding the wire toy with

the mad percussion of their guns.
Like an arrow composed of arrows
the music-skein navigates

by moon and pale pole-star
towards its finale; Bang! Bang! Bang!
feather-white breast-meat, pâté de fois gras –

and still it keeps coming. There's not
a stomach or heart or ideology
can contain it all. Silence

might be the leanest meat,
but I love it when the guitar-bird
stretches it neck and calls.

The Oedipus Experience

(After an outdoor performance of *Oedipus Rex* at Kings College, Aberdeen University, Ma
2000)

A lush-limbed cherry tree – a cloistered cloud –
showered guilt-pink confetti on our hair.
From roof-ridge to ridge, urgent as the chorus'
shrieked grief, the skrill-skrill, skrill-skrill
of oyster-catchers' wordplay stabbed the air.
Seers see and see but when those brooch-bright boles –
where eyes like owls once stared – spilled
their livid petals down your cheeks, who could look?
What had we to offer you but awe –
who fought the blizzards of the inner eye,
the prophecy-birds screaming round your head –
and the futile thunder of applause?
These beating hands and hearts, pink-fleshed, blind,
corruptible as cherries in your mind.

Cuckoo Love

Pre-dawn awakening.
Naked cuckoo-spawn feels
in his sac-lined shell
the muffled rapids
and gush-red falls
of his foster-mother's heart;

in dawning fear
hallucinates ruptures
of her miniature plumbing,
feathery leaks
becoming unstoppable
deluge; and his struggles

to escape are those of
a cat from a sack,
a diver from his helmet,
the mind from its drowning
head; his instincts —
self-preservation and

killing — necessary
as breath.
            When she,
the diminished mother,
flies, is flung from him
and back again to
lose her head in his gullet,

stuffing him full
of life is all life offers.

And she hears
the sing-song mockery
of his call invoking
the heady fruitfulness

of life without recalling
the theft of hers,
there amongst the ripple-
dappled reeds where
her heart all but burst
for the joy of

mothering.
        Dawn
reiterates dawn. Look,
the flung-down shells
of her little ones, gaping
like primitive mouths
before love is born.

On Not Being Able to Embrace Old Age

"I'm yours," she said,
as she undressed.
But when I saw those
shrugged up shoulders
and the corrugations
joining them to
the pointless bags
of her breasts; the slack-slung
folds of her throat;
her splay-fleshed arms;
and between and below
that emptiest of clefts;
I denied her.
                    Though
I wanted to bury
my face there, like a lover,
to breathe her
parchment odours
in perpetuity, I could not;
but posed as a monument
to youth instead, watched
the dropped leaf
of her face crinkle
into a smile,
a cradle of tolerance,
while mine wept.

Warning

It might have been illusion but
the dust stayed put
when her feet kiss-kissed the ground;

and with every walking sway
of her frame a wave
of the stupefied ocean fell down.

It seemed the hair
above her head eclipsed the sun – spirals
of blonde fire glanced off her nape

half-blinding the lookers-on. Away
she hipped it across the sand
in a vision of herself, entering the sea

in her skin to glide
moon-pale amongst its swathes. And the dogs
of life leapt with her – to greet her, to guard

her – no need for speech or entreaty,
each understood.
What more can the literal tongue say?

– real as the gales her lashes stirred
our minds' subliminal morse
blinks from the lighthouse's eye and reports

her printless feet progressing, bubbles
signalling breath under the sea; a wake
of last-gasp divers; drownings; calamity.

*(After a sighting of the mermaid of Zennor at Porthias beach,
West Penwith, Cornwall, on 11ᵗʰ August 1999.)*

Visiting the Volcano

(Lotte Glob, Potter and Ceramic Sculptor,
Durness, Sutherland)

Heading North you see
this mis-shape of a mountain
shimmering like a berg
above the shifting tundra-waves.

You climb its horned hump-
back and weld your flesh
as tightly to it – earth, air,
fire and water – as you dare.

Snow thickens like a skin.
In the skull's melt-rock
your mind's a blue-glass pool,
your limbs are twists of

black like flame-scarred roots.
You know there isn't a blind
star that hasn't flung lances
of light before it died,

and look, in lochans
and at the sea's rim,
like massing turtles
the very stones are floating,

and beast-forms are rearing
from burns and crannies.
As fast as trains winds
rush from between the stars

in the farthest North.
Piece by fought-for piece
mountains are being re-
cycled by Lotte Globb.

Cries from a Clearing

They've dug up another
bog-bound victim
with a 2000 year old
grin in its leather throat.

Time has proved no match for
the acid seep of bog-
juices tanning its little-
girl skin, gentling

these petrified eyelids,
so young, so seeming-live.
The archaeologists, myth-deep
in sphagnum-clods, are elated –

meaning leaks from
her twice-roped throat,
its cave-deep cut,
the punctured cerebellum,

and it's hard not
to long – reverentially –
to finger and kiss
such death-defying flesh.

Who were her loving
murderers? What particular
monsterings of the mind did they
feed her innocence to?

We've mostly sprung from tribes
pragmatic enough to
hang their gods and demons
on sharpened sticks to cry,

to cry for anyone,
like a goat in a clearing;
we can believe this daughter
was sacrificed. But it's

hard not to howl against
the father who'd aspire
to such unspeakable an honour
for his little one.

Lies for Believers

White ones return with greenery,
cooing over stilled oceans.
SEABORNE CIRCUS THWARTS HURRICANE J –
ALL SAVED. J is for Judas, of course,

whose silver whoppers still circulate
like millstones, grinding the bone truth down;
the meal they make is black
as blood-pudding. And then there is

that technicolour eyebrow raised
to the weeping sky like a neon sign,
NEVER AGAIN, DARLINGS, NEVER AGAIN,
constant as mascara in a flood;

and always this daguerrotype
with the monk's hood and blade like a capital D –
for Dunderhead, Dear Dodo,
do you always believe what you read?

In gardens and on bridges,
in the shadows of spires, lips pressed to
soft-drumming jugular veins
tumescent with desire, we've told them all –

and the bitterest are red-and-ochre as,
quill-sharp as, proud-crowned as,
cruel-spurred as, that infamous cock
perched on Peter's thighbone to crow.

Lord Baby

(Dec 25th)

Lord baby if that straw –
for which forgive us – irritates,
it will seem like ladies' thighs –
which He forbids you – after
the rape-by-nails your stars predict.

Feel your frightened mother's
heartbeat stop, whose breasts – glimpsed
in torchlight as the soldiers searched –
you so adore, their tendered nipples
coarsened by rough curses; Lord, who

could still be virgin after this? So
you, Christchild, unbalanced by
desire, will learn the lovely body
is a trap, its twists of muscle
and tendril-tender nerves cocooned

but seething in swaddling rags.
Forgive us the End none of us
can escape – your bouldered cave. Think
of it as a haven like this stable
out of which you will rise into

your self-made parable and cry
a new conscience for the centuries,
you whose pretty mouth sucks
so busily here, as if breast-milk
flowed direct from paradise.

We each define fulfillment and fru-
stration in the image of ourselves –

the body flails in its personal mire.
But when you cry, New Lord,
sharp shepherds and potentates –

even the pillaging soldiery –
shudder like naked sheep and hide
from the fiery question-marks
crazing the sky. May your mother's
milk-flow double and your straw be dry.

Lady

Madonna might have black hair
or blonde; breasts like grapes,
or like hanging planets;
a velvet purse for her mouth
or glistening plums—it

doesn't matter. Oh she sings
and her arms crook
as naturally as cradles; her snood
falls close as night, as sheaves
of hair; so we, her prodigal

children, cling to her. Lady,
chaste as light, fecund as fire,
the orbiting mind might scan
the purest blue
but flesh is its habitat;

because you slip from us –
beyond gender, past belief,
blue where light coagulates,
white where it thins and pours –
we re-invent you; flawless

in holy glass but fleshly
in our heads, tangible
as the fruits we finger in stores.
And our kisses like this... this... this
personifying prayer...

Second Coming

I walked in another man's language
with my hands over my ears, hard rain
smirring its vowels across my eyes,
the whetted appetites of strangers' tongues

flaying me. I was afraid to taste
the meats and salads of its vocabulary,
not knowing the order in which its words are eaten,
waiting with furtive glances to copy their mouthings.

Deaf, blind and hungry at last I knelt
in their holy House and ate their dead God with them –
Hosannahs! Poetry! A babel of stonework falling!
And when I stood exquisite choirs trilled 'Jesus!'

And the Word walked the world and found no borders.
And I, in my ragged coat of translation, stumbled after
crying, "beat me, break me, I understand you all,
your names queue to be born on the tip of my tongue" –

and I walked in the language, tall and purposeful,
an exclamation-mark at the end of each utterance.
And my belly was a waterbutt, my brow a teeming spire,
and I cut commandments in granite with my teeth.

The Big Cat's Pupil

Glamorous accelerating clouds,
panther-vapours pouncing out of summer's
blue filmed sky, complete their illusions;

time expands and contracts like a big cat's pupil
but who needs claws to prove the future's fatal
or tiger's eyes to verify cruel pasts?

Follow me into the circus's brawl and dazzle,
immerse yourself in drum-rolls, brass crescendos,
fixate yourself on the glitter-girl's flung flesh –

oh and fall with her
– feel your very pelt-hairs lift and yowl –
descend from those high-strung chandeliers

with the slowness of a turning autumn leaf
to the rough-roped net; and gasp there
like a hunted down gazelle, the blue deeps

of its eyes filming over, your terror
let loose like a cat in a crowd
blinded by blood and applause.

Clowns tumble the dust.
A pair of white horses prances by.
Can clouds only be cloud, is the present reduced to now,

when the lion in us dies?

From Captain Oates To Captain Scott

Once the door is shut
and the last of life's
snow-flurries has been
dusted off, and your frost-
clogged mittens are hung
on the oven rail, and memories
like the boiler have been
damped down, it will seem
possible to say
"I'm going to stay in,

I might be some time,"
and lock the icedoor
in their faces. There are
corridors tiled like urinals
down which you'll step,
an anxious patient,
off-yellow walls following
the laws of perspective
to a white stop in your mind.
With your gangrenous toes

and fat-stores squandered
it could take forever
to reach it, but you'll
seem to melt through
the minutes like the snow
in that billycan we
couldn't boil, in the lost
outside world of feeling
and weather. The walls are
closing in, piss-yellow

and reeking. Somebody
dressed as a surgeon,
importantly surrounded
by masked women, is
checking a silver
chronometer and beckoning
you on. His lips, cool
and chivvying, will be
the last to kiss you. They'll
taste of Amundsen.

The Song of the Unknown Civilian

in memory of the millions lost to war, 0 – 2000 A.D.

Time, flowering between the stars,
child of the unfulfilled moment,
grant us our nameless place

in the silence between
your second hand's halts on its
metronomic voyage round your face.

Time, now that you have charted
the creases and fault-lines
in the features of all you embrace –

this tumult-crusted earth,
its moon-crazed waters, the ice-
and-sun-scarred flesh of the human race –

ease us as smoothly as river-
flow over that boulder
– grant us such unperturbed grace –

into your measurelessness. Time,
myth-maker that you are, though we share
the unicorn's disgrace –

no identifiable bones, nothing
willed or inherited, lost
from the cumulative gene-pool without trace –

grant our unlisted names
primal-word status – not thoughts, *chimes*
in the foetal brain, *karma* from space.

ORIGINAL MYTHS

Adam

Adam rolls over and plunges
his hand in the burn
to guddle for ice – it's that cold;
plucks out of its rigor-mortis
a weed-haired stone like a heart
– it's that hard – its marblings
numb-white as his nails
and frozen jowls; hugs
it in his armpit for the body-
heat – can't you feel
the sinews? the heart-wall?
the mind in its iced-up freezer?
And trails his lips like snails
on its weed-soured hardness,
kissing, keening in his throat
like a mourner for his brothers
lying in blood-moated
heaps, gash-mouths all over,
brains spilling.
             And his
the only heart beating, his
the only pulse speaking in
drops off a frozen rock,
of life before his death made
stones of us all.
                 After war, and snow-
time, and the fruitless Fall.

Eve

Eve's garden has gone
to the devil. Slug-invaders
digest its innocent shoots.
She wears a tattoo
on her big-D breasts
to discourage guardian angels
– a blue-eyed ball-biting snake;
once offered herself to God
who sent her a brand-new Adam,
this man in mourning. He
kissed as if he'd forgotten
the meaning of flesh, gave her
a clock to measure their
innocent days and a warmed
stone to fondle.
        How she
loved him!
        Nightly she cleaned
his wounds, her breasts hanging
in his sky like new-found
planets; daily he washed her
in thawing blood; hourly
all round them the broken
walls of Eden grew mosses
and lichens, the ice-caps slipped
closer, their hot-house fell
into disrepair, and weeds propogated
like peoples, everywhere.

The Tree

The tree could not know
its purpose; or why, when blight
wormed into its fruit, Adam
whirled round like a storm
and axed it. Everything went
dark. Clocks wound down,
the tree lay down
in its limbs, and a million
unstoppable years chewed it
to mush.
         No-one could know
what they did not know until
Adam woke from his stupor
– choked with love of Eve
but unable to remember – on
the planet's fermenting floor;
and saw that the tree
was pulped smooth as paper,
and penned in bright blood
his heart-pounding poem *"Eve,
naked as despair, "* – giant-
slaying couplets shot straight
from a sling – and ran
with his scrolled-up words
to the broch by that
brackish burn where Eve
milks serpents, and yearns.

Babel

Have you been there?
the Ark must have sounded
like this at feeding times.
Eve welcomed him back
like a fish-wife, flayed him
with her fishtail tongue,
set the hollow walls wailing
with slappings of tongues,
the trills and gutturals
of passion-torn tongues, the twistings
of tongues passing all
understanding...
    And the broch still stands –
have you been there?
                  Adam dis-
lodged one heart-sized stone
and rolled it like a sweet-
meat into her mouth,
cooed his new rhymes to her,
stooped to lather her
comfortless feet, made honey
of her; for forty days
and forty moon-touched nights
made Eden for her –
a Time-Before-War
of doves and brown-limbed rivers
where every beginning begins.
Have you been there?

Divisions of Labour

"She loves me, she loves me
not." Adam is lying
log-like on Solomon's couch
massaging his heart. Eve
is squatting and retching
into the burn, her changelings,
about to arrive,
swelling like mad ideas –
as out of control.
"How much can be borne
by one stone planet
with no choice but to blunder
round the sun?" Adam asks,
while Solomon reads the runes
and sharpens his blades.

    I tell you Eve's screams
were enough to curdle
her own breast-milk, to set
one child at another's throat
in the womb.
              "O God
where is your wisdom?"
Solomon cried as his sword
dropped through their skulls
and four spines rose, gathered
their armies of bone, and scattered
to each corner of the sky.

Fruit Picker

"There are 'suitable' occupations –
like scrubbing the pantaloons
of your harem trollops;
stockpiling salt for souring
their sugar-plum nipples; grinding
Rhinoceros Horn, oh stutter-
lipped lord, to stiffen
the wrinkled-up sock of your
resolve on those spittle-
drenched nights after peppers
and hooch with the boys – sweet
Cain and noble-browed Abel –
dread nights you 'save' me for;
but I need more."
                    She turns
from the glittering artifice of
his eyes to a sky stretched
so transparently blue you could
swear you'd glimpses of angels.
She walks and barley fields part
like waves of an ancestral sea,
she walks and the red
earth sustains her. And hers
is the warmth, and hers
are the waters, hers
these husbanded tree-roots. And hers
is the reward; Forbidden Fruit.

Gamblers

Adam is dicing with Samson
between the sky-hefting
pillars of the temple.
"Have you seen the rivers
of gazelle creating perpetual
motion on the burnt-sienna plain?"
Delilah whispers to Eve,
reaching for her scissors,
invoking migrations of muscle
under Samson's tawny skin.
The dice are as loaded as
the Natural Selection game,
the dance of the Dominant
Genes, begun when Adam
and Eve's tensed thighs French-
kissed beneath the trees.

    Adam plays blind but Eve,
tortured by Samson's vulnerable
eyes, forsees the pillars
tumbling and his knotted shoulders
breaking; how futures can be trans-
formed as fast as angels falling,
or slow as the ceaseless trek
from amoeba to brontosaurus,
from axe to atom bomb.
And her mind can find no home.

Flood

"I'd like to introduce to you
the abacus of bones" –
Adam in professorial mode
the day that yeasty waters
half-drowned their broch,
and Noah created history
in his ark of gopher-
wood by saving the zoo.
    Eve felt Adam counting
the days and nights of down-
pour on their kissing ribs,
down her spine like a tickle,
spider-light under her breasts,
trespassing round her nipples
and forgetting...
              How many
orbits of those massy moons
before it occurs to Eve
that this floodtide of
delight might be improved?
Fingering his fig-leafed bits
she said, "God plucked
this rib and hung it
between your thighs to
ignite promissory rainbows
in my eyes..."
            "Flood?" said
Adam to Noah, "what Flood?"

Plague

Where are all the men?
Have Joseph's dream-locusts
fallen like Philistine armies
on our golden fields of men?
Turned our rivers of men
to blood and a plague of crows
to strut the bone-strewn
acres of our men? Lying
in the tatters of their flesh
and bone, there in the fruit-
less fields where war is
a locust-swarm swallowing the
golden stubble of our men?
    They fell out of the four
black corners of the sky,
familiar as husbands and sons,
demonic as angels, lethal
as firebrands in a haystack.

                          And

oh we stood like statues
of ourselves, wound in the sun's
iron bands, watching
what our minds forbade us
to see.
    And still stand, wind-
turned monuments to faithfulness,
pillars of salt holding no-one,
beside a murdered sea.

Tears

When Eve weeps, her tears
turn to chamber-stopping
boulders sealing in
the mummies of lost innocence;
sweet-fleshed still,
bound in serpent-skins.
Now she is weeping
in the drench-walled broch
with a paper in her hand,
white paper in her hand,
and rage like a raven
stropping its beak
on her spine.
          Adam's
poems were once the darlings
of her days. Chanting
in shade or in evening sun
he'd interweave such words,
so tendril-light of touch,
so vine-like in her hair,
that new fruits grew; or tease
her with such hintings that
new meanings moved like
fingers on her flesh.
            All, now
she has fathomed the drift
of his enchantments, rapacious
as the smiles of any snake.

Poem for Eve

"Goodbye, good friend, go
dry-eyed into your house.
Arrange yourself in the vase
of it and flower. You move
like a long-maned palamino,
you grace the fields you graze
with beauty and latent power.
You spit the bit from your mouth,
you always will.

              No flower
I've seen is more itself
than you. Flower and be
proud of your silk skin,
your charged scent, the laden
curves of your leaf-limbs
and cupped blooms, the light
reflected back when your nape
is bent to catch the last
of the day from your window-sill.
    I never swam in the waterfall
or pushed through the waist-
high barley of your hair; I
never will. You are
the lover I never knew
the wife I never took,
my uncut stook. Remember
how much this friend cared."

Hero

This is their finest hour.
Adam and his Sherpas
have crawled off the mountain
on buckling knees, God's
weighty new commandments
cut into the headstones
on their backs. What's left
to achieve?
          But though the planet
is a storm of ticker-tape
and Adam's star-strung name
will outlast speech, rumours
have wormed their way in.
"Is it true," they whisper
to Eve, "that Adam genu-
flected to a burning bush?
Did he make them haul
an Ark of Relics over
foothill, ridge and crevasse?
Have forensic tests proved
the immutable slabs
are blank as burn-smoothed
stones? And, delirious
and weak, did Adam try to
take off from the summit
with an olive-branch in his teeth?
What should we believe?"

God

God couldn't find a way
to stay in one piece.
His voice broke and fled
into bushes and clouds;
his flesh disguised itself
as mouthfuls of bread;
his blood turned to wine,
his hands fell to splinters,
his temples grew twisted horns.
      And his ribcage hung
like a beast's on a butcher's
hook.
      And Adam nailed
God's image in the broch
next to his own, and Eve's,
and all their progeny's,
the peoples of the blue-
veined Earth all nailed to
one family tree. And God
was pleased.
            But peoples flower
like weeds – Adam's
collection of portraits out-
grew space and their tree
pushed into heaven –
                        a study
of Salome, her hips describing
circles as subtly as any
serpent's, took God's place.

Brothers

Adam meets his brothers
where the burn swells the river,
there where the river
vomits into the sea.
His brothers lie with him,
they conjour up for him
the snakepit in his stomach,
the venom in Eve's.

    Eve runs to the ancient orchard
but it has petrified, lies
seedless as her own womb
since the flood; she
pounds on Solomon's door
but the Queen of Sheba's
tongue is in his ear;
she runs to the temple
but Samson has pulled it down,
and Delilah is chasing
shadows on the plain.

    And when the eldest brother
grapples her to the ground
Eve bites his Adams apple.

    And they take Adam's heart
and sling it at the sun – it
hangs there like an eye-mote
no-one can weep away.

TEN FLOORS DOWN

Keats's First Love

As if some latent disease
or virus the blind brain nurtured
had completed its maturation,
corrosive as desire, slow but fatal.
Everything life promised him was innocent
as that moist-lunged intake of air
before the infected kiss – which he
had practiced in the recesses
of his poems and lip-smudged mirror
till his red mouth ached. *"Promise"*,
he breathed, and she did, his tongue
already at play in the forks of her flesh;
while love, our commonest cancer,
deconstructed the contents of his head.

Art Forever, 2002

Her minimilist canvases became mirrors
on which breathed air propagated cancerous moulds –
their soft-spliced shifting water-drifts
smirred the hard-edged mindscapes
we exist in, but couldn't prevent her
seeing. So she started using stones
to fracture the glass, and then its shards –
still flashing fragments of our world –
to carve unintelligible symbols in her skin.
So she bled for art,
so hacked her path to wealth and accolades,
her severed limbs, and ears, and nose, and tongue
staining our gallery walls like relics of martyrs,
her hung-up eyes permanently outstaring as all.

Guernica, 1937

And what about Picasso
wrestling the bull of Espana
into perspective, the flung limbs
and conflagration of screams
– animal, vegetable, mineral –
fighting to be released from his head.
His head, a 20th century
dome of driven thought,   burnt
to a leather skull-cap over a monkey's
black-eyed face, all instinct
and cunning. But it wasn't an artist
who butchered Guernica under the sun,
he just re-lived it – from every eye's agonized
angle – then exploded it like a bomb.

Impossible Perfection

Then there's Rainer Maria Rilke, eyes
popping with longing, consumed by
impenetrable mirrors, like suns. See, his panther
is being devoured by the disc
of its own yellow eye, as if a blindness
of angels, more complete than the cumulative
sight of all gone creatures, had demanded
impossible perfection. Neither the love

of women nor of reflecting Christ
– corruption, God knows, to the core –
can compete with such Other-Beingness.
Self is its ringing glass, shattered,
a black hole churning the world in its belly;
and art its angel of untouchable immensity.

Emily Dickinson in Love

I see it like this – a rock arrives
on her front porch and puts on a display
of pyrotechnics as stupendous as the Northern Lights
then rolls on its way, having first contrived
a trail of poppers and fizzers as its finale.
Or some snake trances new patterns in the grass
on a day so still a spinster can hear
her heart making boom down the valley.
How many times must she hear it
before night arrives with the chloroform,
or the snake unstraps its chainmail
and heads off home? How can she bear it
when that plank in Reason gives way
and plummets her 10 floors down into poetry?

You Don't Have to Be

You don't have to be a scientist,
or poet, my Best, to express
the ordinary accident of love.
Every early morning the gist
of what the birds sing
is *thinking's for academics*,
flexing their metacarpals
and ticklish primaries, pulling
the sky over them like a glove.
This morning we're two swifts
and the science of aerodynamics
exists solely to lift
us above the clouds and record the swooping marvels
of mindlessness.